Labour of Love
by Boogie Bonét

Written by Boogie Bonét
Cover Art by Tarn Ellis
Copyright © 2022 Boogie Bonét
All rights reserved

Boogie Bonét has asserted her right to be identified as the author of this
Work in accordance with the Copyright, Designs and Patents Act 1988

Independently published

ISBN 9798578434631

dedication

to my nan, Cislyn

the matriarch and the medicine

the woman who's prayers protected me before i would pray for myself

the one who crossed oceans alone in search of a better life

even for those of us
she could not yet imagine

thank you for being brave first

because of you,

i'm brave enough to choose me

contents

introduction

life is a journey.

i spent the first quarter feeling like i was here to be scored. i didn't realise that this existence was merely a visit, and a choice that i made to journey. being born into a world that moulded my experience outside of alignment with nature sent me spiralling. so, i've been working on getting myself back, and noticing what was lost. what was lost, was love.

i had neglected to nurture love within myself.

i searched through acts of sadness and trauma, and through acts of abuse. i found the firstborn that carried the weight of the world on her shoulders, on her back, and on her head. i saw life through her eyes and it was gloomy. i held her like she was my daughter and reminded her that she's worthy. i told her each eye she found undeniable beauty in was a portal reflecting pureness that was her own. i promised to help her find her way back to love by going through the labour of it.

as i flow deeper into the loving peacefulness that is remembrance, i couldn't leave the old girl behind without sharing her final labour.

that she was

zero to five percent
chance my womb would have
to hold you
fathomably unfair
yet fairness is not pledged
truth be told
it is unfairness of this journey
which made a warrior out of me

pain has riddled
far too long
to remember painlessness
enough to say
this was chosen for self

is the discomfort of not knowing you
that pinches the nerves
that make me sleep less

so, take me

from scars etched by sorrow
carried in the temple of my womanhood

free the land in me
that will lay at the feet of my
seeds who must roam free
must meant to be

to know i gave chance
is a purpose that cannot escape

~ *endometriosis*

i will love you through your
impermanence –
in my every act
    and if not meant to meet in the
space of my temple,

    will hold your spirit
  in the hands of my heart
until the beginning of eternal time

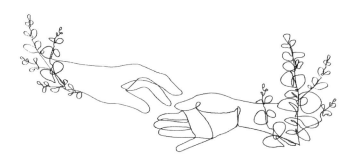

~ *spirit babies*

i learned to mother myself
when told by a doctor
the only child my womb may carry
is trauma

eleven days,
        in eleven months
promised i'd lose your siblings
before we'd meet

science didn't know
our family unites
higher

and not only shall you manifest,
        but in birth
will the spirit of your sister
        bloom through your feet

~ *broken promises*

the secrets i kept
saved every life
but my own

~ you're welcome

i used to be a child of destiny
what hostage it was
to hold self in survival
feet planted on chairs
wore necklaces of rope
awaiting natures push
far too afraid to kick
rightly so
refusing to give up the pressure
laid bare on my collar bones
and give life a try
was never ready to die
barely suicidal if honest
just afraid to
thrive
i wonder how many times
the gust of wind forced feet
heavier than i wear
over edges
of finality
those like myself
simply too afraid to blossom
now life will forever tell it that
their meaning belongs to self-slaughter
don't know why luck greeted me
but haunted by it still
as even now i barely prosper
to get here had to hang up the will of survival
a chore for more wondering
maybe those sucked off the face
of today into tomorrow
those with courageous kicks
knew that to die is the only way
to be alive

~ God isn't ready for us yet

there is a piece of my heart that lives in a
luxurious land
numbness is its name
does not dance nor smile
just is
completely unaffected by all
it is times like this
i wish to climb into her
wrap my knees into my chest
a ball of flesh
screaming her awake from the depth
of detachment
"you do not get to feel nothing
while the rest of us dies before you"
only she understands it most
as before numb was her playground
she was the embodiment of the ocean
feeling everything
and it killed her

~ *i remember*

the fear of man was the thief that
set my spirit into a womb of worry
who could i?
if not frightened into this plane?

cried barely
under the acceptance of a
doomed fate
that carried me to lose it all
the fright
   the survival
      misguidance, too

dropped a jewel or few in the whirlwind
found that God will shade a runaway
   from the darkness of a chasing past
     even if a once-a-slave is brave enough to
        rummage back through the trauma
          and retrieve emeralds

sometimes in this shade
my body
 scores my other senses
the smell of fear that follows
is pungent
   and undeniable is the scent of
    what has haunted for
a lifetime

somehow i blink and awaken to light
    a pocket full of diamonds
each time

  i wouldn't lean on faith
if my life depended on it
til the divine knocked on my heart
said "*hand it over*"

traded me a piece of intention
plus a promise
to carry me past the last demons
every time wicked blinks its evil eye

~ *lucky*

was enough
when pierced skin with razors just to feel

enough
   with a tongue tasting salt
distinguishing rain from tears

 as heart whaled into oceans
still enough
    as given to God

whilst memories seek
to write sentences of past into present
 never not enough

for the Highest
        to work through me

~ *always enough*

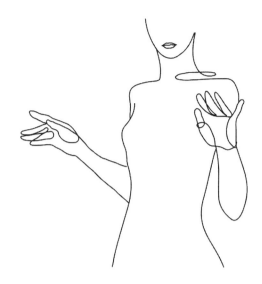

nestled in the sheets
are words unsaid
i offer them centre stage
only in dreams
as i wake
they scoff
 once silenced
 now the silencer of myself

~ *self abused*

retained in a deafening world
she did not hear her thoughts
until distractions showed up
parting deception to silence
and horns of remembrance
pierced present time
nothing but screams escaped her
from that day forward
she never looked at anybody
the same again

~ *psychotic awakening*

i love my father enough
to stop pretending
my life
did not hurt

~ *it's strange to be estranged*

first born

sirens in the distance
  never came close enough
to hear my whispered pleas

each time the lights pass me by
i hear babies
drowning under bedsheets
in hopes of a closer siren

i never get close enough
to save them

~ *i had to save me first*

what if justice is just this
finding peace alone
with accountability that will never truly be claimed
guardians that don't love you more than they feel shame
less shame is to feel guilt
then replace with blame
onus is not a trait
in the dna
that runs through every
weepers veins, too
somewhere along the way
my innocence was traded for agony
i wonder which material item
placed above my needs
was bought for
the trade of my virtue
wonder too,
if without the pain paying for my testimony
would i have ever been
of any value?

~ *all she does is daydream*

first born blues
burdened at the cost
of every hood of development
the day you learn not to wait for sorry
is the day all apologies thereafter
become
void
until nothing even matters
but oh
it all does

~ *it all does*

i was a helpless little girl
with dreams bigger than the
way i saw out
playgrounds filled with lawyers and doctors,
teachers, dancers
people that would grow to smoke or drink
their lives away
i ran on no sleep,
4am nosebleeds
and a need to prove i was more than
an invisible mistake
there was no time to see myself past grief
today the proof is in my step
i am seen
time is abundant
and it is nothing
i should've prayed to live
beyond the paths
i could not see for myself
as still, i have not passed grief
i'm just the hopeless aftermath
of a hopeless child
still waiting for something to give

~ *grief's companion*

a smoky scent
only escaped through
portal of
confrontation
"keep your demons off me"
hushed in invisible tones.
in higher realms,
my angels slay which you worship
under the dark cloud of you
i remember
to get the knife
first
next time

~ *washing powder*

i knock paradise's door
with my veracity
sad waters of heartache
bleed by my side
my beat feels no ease
stiff blind to see what was done unto me
without igniting flames
to rid the left behind and
give rise to a new dimension
a thing must got to give
i did not weather storms
to succumb to they who
could only claim fame
if murdered my soul
even in fury
my pupils are the only thing i set ablaze
for having to fight so long
so alone
yet never lonely
for a painful journey never seizes
to walk by my side

~ misery's favourite company

the first time i gave birth i was three
i had already met loss
but it didn't meet me
a comrade with soft eyelids
arrived through mama's womb
our front row seats sat on diametric ends
we conceptualised a harmonising tune
i don't know who was more afraid
the sisters or the façade
eight years delayed
the bloom we shared
she favoured soft eyes
except was grounded on little legs
they marched past the fear
that lived before her
scripted us a broadway classic
that almost rewrote history
'til i broke character
together we are old enough to
rebirth our mother
if we were born in time
would've nested her away
until life was not cruel
perhaps once i trade my pain
we can afford to

~ *spice and sci-fi*

time used to stop in the doorway
of a tiny little flat on alcester
i would step out of my body
just to edge her to say something
she was always frozen in fright
for far too long
time she opened her mouth to speak
it took five tries for a whisper to turn
to a pointless screech
i go back to alcester whenever
fear makes a mockery out of me
on the outside looking in
it's a victory when i use my voice
they've learned not to expect a sound
from miss meek and mild
their lack of expectation
keeps me glued to guilt
and i know it wasn't my fault
but you can't tell me that

~ *i was just a child*

my grandmothers hand
warned away jinn
when she dripped
agua de kananga
across my temple
sheltered my nostrils
and made me inhale the God
yeye could no longer sea
then guided
my palms to tongue
prayers
that spared
me the day i walked
into shadows
under the sun

~ nanny's number

ironic of humble beginnings
to cause a rage in the lives of
little buds

to bloom heirs
in concretes of destruction

some slip through
cracks
others never meet chance

'til it's too late to replant
the flower
cemented in histories pavement

~ *war against children*

i used to be haunted by
nightmares when i slept
  and tortured by demons
    when i woke
i still haven't quite learned to
tell the difference
between
  heaven
    and hell

~ *oneness*

i laughed through tears
when my name fell to its feet pridefully
from lips declaring me a champion
the hold of a hand shaking well done
made the finale flash before my eyes
and it was more fetching than
the medal placed around my neck

as i guarded my trophy cabinet
watching my name glisten
like my golden child
i pictured it in lights like taina
i could be anything i wanted
and when the tone turned sour
and hostility retreated me to my room
i talked to ladybirds on the window ledge
with my lids sealed
together with the backing of
dayna's vocals
we held the vision

it wasn't bad until retrospect
because even when actions
introduced me to contradictions
my parents always showed me
i could be a paradox
and still earn trophies

~ *karate kid*

strange men
gold teeth grins
ambience of cannabis drenched tables lingers
a kid my age eyes me
'fore counting more twenties in the corner
they always said i was big now
naïve kin miss the tone behind
eyes that would torment an 8-year-old
then cry seduction in court
pitiful perverts
i sliced my eye
left them a
see-right-through-you
on my way out
and hoped the boy
pocketed some paper
the powder too
kicked it to the streets
when the options are few
better a pusher
than groomed to a predator

~ *they're all sick*

holding seconds
savouring freedom already lost in a verdict to come
remaining illusionary is the luxury of
being without sentence

a delay does not suffice
breath grips
chest tight

puts misery into me
waiting for chance
to countdown the clock
of life

one day i will breathe again
a day far from today
where docks overflow with families
whilst i sit on my kitchen floor
with a final grasp on my sanity

a wedge in my heart says
i will gain my life's first regret
for not being where
judgment determines
a fate i cannot fight

God calls his child
and holds her fragility before her eyes
responds,
"you know you better"…

    …

    … six thousand,
   two hundred
 and
five days

~ *til i'll breathe again*

sitting on the brighter side of a nightmare
that one cannot wake from
is not a seat of royalty

to be above ground
whilst one's heart has been lowered
to lay beneath
is not to sit on a throne

the impression of callousness
chills through my body
yet aware that its cold warmth
is no comparison to
the ice-cold vessel
of a mother's sacred seed

still, i mourn

and shall continue in soundlessness

for my mourning is not allowed
in the court realm of society

"bring back the death sentence…
for the family too"
they smear their refusal of compassion
for the lesser loss
that still breathes

the loss of a verdict that
denies a wealth of reasonable doubt
a loss fair to a stranger
called justice

leaves a hole in the heart of sisters
left out of the know
"when they see us" lingers in the air
and seers seek not obliviousness
but beg for impartial truth

always in silence

as on the darker side of this nightmare
is a mother's plea for an undoing
that will never be heard
an exoneration impossible
at least, must be returned
the minimum of an unfulfilling justice

it is to suffer
to love a soul so much
that the choice
to be
guilty by association
is a privilege chosen
just to hold them close

~ *there is no bright side*

i pray my daughter never walks in
on those late nights
where the wounds resurface
and i'm too weak to tend them
nights where i lay in my blood
too frail to conceal my burdens
with a strong cloak
i pray she never tries to console me
in moments that mark her
with inflictions of my past
pray my shame
never becomes me
in moments i cannot avoid
and swears my girl to silence

~ *sorry in advance*

Labour of Love

homegirl cries
but tears do not fall
for they know better than to gloss over
the grief she must conceal

such is life

that son's birthed
by black women
belong to the system
of demolishing hearts

instil fear and bring life to
tragedy
death to kings at royal hands
crowned in an unawareness that denies heirs right

hushed burdens respond to women
who cry as streets claim ownership of seeds
nurtured and bloomed within sacred wombs

'til accountability demands her to sign
a cheque for a barrister or coroner
chosen by the side of grief that
life has her child fall
all the while, homegirl knows
across from her experience
is a mourning sister placed in opposition

for hers, by yours

for yours, by hers

~ *the game of life*

the deeper meaning to life
is lost in the glamour of strife
masking pain as the qualifier
      for riches

taught freedom much too late
children are born to create
early tombs
  to mirror wombs
of the women fathers called bitches

silence is the suffering
the man of the house uses, to
quiet screams

rich black eyes are worn by mothers
   reflecting the expense of love
  that takes away a daughters dreams

of possibility,

a remembrance of a calling
making adolescent tricks feel worth the falling...
for, a thousand times
life had me die on its surface

pierce flesh, bleed almost to death
think suicide is to be of service

we fear not God but man,
o' no wonder that we can
only see consequence in last breaths
not in each action welcoming
souls death

do you think we live to cry?
watch blood pour from our mothers eye?
be weighed into graves by burdens…

look into eyes of peers,
see serpents?

must we lose our way
to find we all have a righteous path bearing our name?

is the price of purpose costed by guilt,
worry,
and shame?

a world created of the Divine,
riddled with curses
that often misalign
from the truth

of one of one
   is one of all

a knowing equating to birth right

only remembered after we're at loss of sight
that the deeper meaning of life

   is not deep at all

it is as simple as our childish dreams
but that is never how it seems
  to the offspring handed nurturing
batons of delusion

~ *writing poems with my brother*

blood on my pinafore does not belong to me
in fact, i belong to her
she who bleeds
i belong too, to he who forced it from the nostrils
of the most beautiful face he'd fail to keep
what have i born into?
a question my eyes will ask for twenty-six years
before realising
the answer is quite possibly hell
where i reside,
fathers wet the head of their child's birth
with an alcoholic beverage amongst pals
christian baptism has priests wetting new-born domes
with water they claim to be holy
but in my hole, my ancestor
wet his firstborn daughters dress with the blood of her queen
mother, whom froze into a shock lasting
two more daughters & eleven years
as for me—E,
i'd only been womb-free for less months than three
before endlessly
embarking on a return to she-
doesn't-know-who-the-f-self-is,
even if only for this reason specifically
only God knows
her, and why earth didn't get to
before there was blood on my pinafore

~ *the life that chose me first*

worthy

it was the last straw when i began
to even fear
justice

~ *carmen and joe*

a bloody tongue
sobbed to me this morning
said
"bite me no more"
and i realised
it's not okay
the deceit i accept
liars i oath my intimacy to
friends
    that were never friends
that the blood on his hands
stain my pen
each time i seek to
write lullabies
turn them to
  misery
sometimes nothing matters
but when everything does
i bite hard

~ *battered tongue*

i learned the language of love
to speak to you
   and in your absence
 found the mother of my orphaned tongue

            she doesn't like you much.

~ *runner*

simply naïve
i trade my senses
for a love bomb
no hissing to alert
my heart faces jeopardy
til out of ashes
again,
i rise

~ phoenix

i went on a date with a stranger
we spoke about God
i was greeted with respect
by shopkeepers who turned their noise at me
because the man i was with was a star
he showed me the world through his eyes
i showed him my dance moves
to the music playing
from a bar across the street
we laughed until our bellies ached
in one evening
i was more alive than i ever felt with you
then you showed up
and committed yourself to the moment
like you attach yourself to every man that takes my gaze
from the post trauma of you
and when he asked what was on my mind
i began to bite my speech
and his ocean blue eyes
turned green
the wittiest jokes lost their humour
and sweat roofed my optics
until i was no longer sure
it was his voice petting my ears
i couldn't bear to face his lips
to see what fell from them
but i know that snicker
was yours
you always do this
keep your word in riddles
when you swore i'd always be yours
you damned me
now i am haunted
forever

~ *familiar spirit*

i give you my hand to hold

God puts the whole world in your hands

you would've caught me
if only you'd see
there is no difference

~ *maybe not*

contagion of desire
if you're not enough
neither am i
i saw you hide your feelings
under the bed you waste your life in
so i waited for you to fall into the
distraction of your insecurities
and hid my ambition next to the shoe box
i thought you'd like me better
if reduced to the vision
you'd caged yourself to
but i failed to quieten
the ticks of life passing me by
the restlessness of waiting
made my pores weep
you drowned me head first in
the buckets of my potential
i tried to get you to see your own
all i wanted was to be enough
a shame you couldn't get over that
i was more than

~ *migraines*

if loved for money alone
would not love you who is poor
the appeal of a noose would diminish
as your shiny jewels made up for

fazes me none
that you please the eyes of strangers
drink wine on the dime of men who afford to swipe blind
if you bared your soul to me
what would i find

if i touch your chest
will i meet the beat of a heart beneath its surface
will your words be true
or used to kindle gas on my furnace
do your lust over your own charm
that you must dim every light brushing your cracks
are you afraid of alarms
that display when you're the one who isn't all that

if i fall, will i be caught in a web of lies
or a delicacy unashamed to apologise
will i whisper to friends
to not ruffle your feathers
because your advantage takes pleasure
in silencing me when we're together

a blessing i do not love for ifs
but for how's of the Divine

how the world becomes a better place
when you help remove dust
that leaves another to shine

how a mother tongue saves
offspring not yet born
so in life they rise
rather than decline

how i can tell my story
then women like me
will leave lames like you
behind

~ *i don't love blind*

God saved her for him
but when he found her, he ran

"because he　　　　*doubted God?"*

because he　　　　had loved her in his dreams for so
long,
to　　　　wake to the reality of her would be
to abandon his desire

~ *too much of a good thing*

seat your admiration at a distance
that allows me to muse in peace
it is already a bellyful
to be an object
rare in design
expected to have no humanity
  to be jolted at every intriguer
skimming my shore
with curious eyes

to be an original imprint
is to be aware that the western
deem you a myth
a wound almost as sore
as mistaking man singing your praises
with his hook and line at the ready
as your own refection at the top of the waters

the difference between a muse
and a mortal
is the one cast out into folklore
sees the sacred root they're preyed for in everything
and reveres it enough to
protect it

you sit above land in restricted superiority
seeing nothing past an idea
worth finding your soul
for a taste

until face to face,
risen to the surface
in answer of the love that lured me

i meet the back of a runner
fleeing the intimidation of awakening

i've been here enough times to know
in the face of truth
people like you choose the world

even at the abandonment of your own soul
found, at the edge of my ocean

~ *don't flatter yourself*

"she's an artist,
after all.

she could excuse him
into
a
masterpiece."

~ *green foliage*

you say it is a mistake
that the arousal of your love
guided me to baptise in
the wells of the Beloved
and ask you to meet me there
i brought holy water from
my surrender
back to your fountain
you did not drink
i too was once afraid
it was you who peeled
fingers from my eyes
and held me to see
divine reflection
in olive mirrors
behind myself
i saw angels
they whispered
i had to submit past your skin
if the arms of the One
were to hold us both
i chose to fall for you
with the Beloved's blessing
the day i realised
you did not want to be my lover
you wanted to be my God
and i'm sorry, my love
that home has a tenant

~ *visitors are welcome*

"*i wouldn't lie to you*", he said
eyes deep in her gaze

a tear danced
to the bow of her lips

before parting to ask

"so, what was that?"

~ *lying king*

sometimes i'd take you back
when i recall our private pranks
before folding them back into place
when i sweep myself into extended isolation
i'm evoked to the way you beheld me
seductively ill-omened
i scroll the lines of time they manufacture
to keep us stuck
find that same face
amongst our mutual friends
and wish i didn't know that reaching out
would be a losing game
i thumb through my children's journals
and see entries enthused by you
feel ashamed that
once i sought you as their father
still picture it on days
life defeats me
sometimes i'd take you back
and take it all away
my connection to Source
dreams inducted to fruition
hang the phone off the hook so
sacred callings stand snubbed
sometimes i bump into your surveillance
and spiral to the brim of sanity
before catching myself adding to a police log
that probably won't save my life
i guess i don't know my worth after all

~ *what is worthy?*

light the gas
shatter her mind to pieces
distracting the lover
    to rape her soul

the mark of the beast is left
by entitled hands
who flick pocketknives
        to the womb
grab throats in false liability

and scream deceptive promises of their death
    at the thought of losing grips

a smirk behind tears that do not fall
 from any eyes but hers
watch her breathless stance
stumble
to save
    his soul that is not lost

but chooses to dance in front of demons
    with the offering of
a mother of the earth
in tow

nothing happened according to the mouth
that spits falsities
    and sits underneath eyes that speak mind games

she weeps at the misbelief of her madness
    into the very arms that would
        murder-suicide her hope away
if ever a saviour sought to pull
  wool from her eyes

in a heartbeat

if only his heart could beat

she might be able to walk away

~ *domestics*

foolishly she believed
it'd end with roses
when all he was willing
to feed her
were
thorns

~ cheap love

i feared i created the red flags
making you appear
like
them
     that i misunderstood your soul

  somewhere in codependency
i convinced myself that my insecurities
moulded you
into those that gifted me mine

i ran into my heart the other day
   she held out her hand, and
      sitting in the palm was my intuition

"*look*"
  she said,

it told me
of all the things i have birthed
the redness of a flag
  was never one

she cursed the desperation out of me
    called her a liar, and
        summoned a vanishing act

she left me to bear witness
to your insecurities
as they ate my soul

you are like them

in fact

you are the
worst them
of
them
all

because you knew me better

~ *red at its most potent*

if even lazy could walk
the procrastinator would not stop
searching for dreams
down the neck
of his mother's wine bottles
to find more disrespect
to spit at me

~ *just another day*

you asked me if i liked women
when i stopped scavenging for your
tasteless crumbs
i heard your burnt ego
handed me a rainbow
in the story that wormed your way
into the pants of other women
it would caress your facade
if those tales spoke true
if i cached a closet
that stemmed my disgust of you
outside of your own actions
maybe you would sleep
without muttering my name
into the sheets of every fling
if your lies concealed
that behind your manly shelter
lives a dark feminine
at war with my light
and you spit accusations
every time she catches a whiff
of me falling more in love
with myself

~ *the other woman*

melancholy skies overhead
self-imprisonment
closing in
love is glum
when it denies itself
at the expense of
a dream manifested
sometimes in silence
i hear your heart
calling
i lay in hope
of a promise fulfilled
at the end of the line
you never finish your sentence
and i'm left tracing fingers
over the guilty breathe
that undertones every smile
i put on your face
you should've told me
you were
leaving

~ *confessions pt. ii*

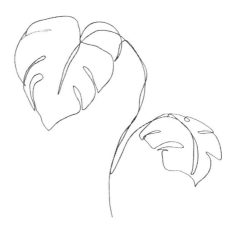

dancing in the graveyard
laughing at the familiar faces
circling me in
my twisted nerves
fought fire with aim
clawed out from under
the dirt of their shame
retrieved my worth
from my womb
and counted how many truths
i'd have to spill to
kill bill

~ *the truth will dig your grave*

one day
as it all falls down
the warmth of a stranger
will kneel beside me
say *"missed one"*
with the piece
to mend my heart
in hand
be nothing familiar
but everything right
and i will be scared
straight
into surrendering
        to love

~ *last man standing*

a pair of spaceship eyes
abduct me to fifth dimensions
where i've resided
in past lives
i hear that i have loved you
in history
memory
in spirit
vowed my heart
eternally
to the familiarity of
your essence
and there is no ocean wide
to make me doubt
i will remember you

~ *seas apart*

find her way back

"*how do you write a poem?*"

i take an honest tongue to God.

~ *prayer is poetry*

somewhere before this battlefield
i learned wrong and right
carried the feeling
into this skin
remembered it
even when
forced my mouth closed
around the joy of devil's secrets

alone i spat out my frustrations
of fear being all it takes
to let wrongs
lead your life

rights become dreams

purpose become dreams desire

sanctuary within to feel out of reach

peace never to be still

until

~ *eventually*

in this moment
i feel my way through the sadness
that sits outside denial's door
awaiting my gaze
for so long i sought acceptance
in rooms
and hearts
that were fully occupied
with desires that did not favour me
i chose to play the losing game
oathing my love to misters
and sister-friends
that sang the most beautiful lullabies
full of lies
i ate them up and wondered
why even when full of a loner's seeking
my stomach starved
i have been empty for a lifetime
deaf to the sound of my own tears cry
i hear them now as they weep
still, my hand only reaches far enough
to deliver handkerchiefs outside of windows
leaving my fragile heart to tend to its own wet face
i want to be okay with holding me every day
but on the ones i forget to remember
i am too weak to face what i have done to her
just like them

~ *the girl at the lake*

most exquisite elements
of my art piece
i paint in
invisible ink
courageous only in that
another with my vision
will read the lines
others fail to see
a coward like everyone
who ever left me
with a secret to hold
as i run from the noise of
living my escape in bold

~ *holding secrets still*

sitting in the corner of my couch
in the distraction of my
neighbours argument
the stillness of being too much
peaks out of me
asking to be shaken
a life of scoffing over emptiness
almost sounds appealing
and i accept one last scream
before stomping my foot to let them have it
to them i have it all
alone in an apartment
they never hear anything from
apart from a silencing footstep at 3am
they say i'm above them
past the literal obviousness
i laugh
they have no idea that
after they leave this quarrel behind
i will gain a week of flashbacks
that leave me cowering at night
and the reason they never hear a sound
is because i can't let the demons know i live here

~ *the victim next door*

never could she fathom
illness
past her own paranoia
looking back at her
i wish foresight traded her
hardened heart
for a hardened tongue
raised her martial fist
and showed the apple
didn't fall far from its tree
the irony
even in need
she knew better than that

~ *don't retaliate*

there is no veil
to conceal fraudulence
that creeps at cracks surface
choking its way in with dishonesty
only illusions near are tales
born in minds of
betraying brethren's
that merit themselves on tactics
and do not notice the loss of their prey
until completely out of reach
along this path
i replaced my need to please
with the praise that flows
mutually
between genuine peers
exalted a shield of protection
around sacred union
and offered you the combination
b-o-u-n-d-a-r-i-e-s
you chose to bypass
on the day you return with your key
find i've changed the locks
make it be your last
and don't come round here no more

~ mildred was a vampire

i'm sorry you didn't get to live for yourself
that your happy ever after was not behind
the door you chose
if i was your companion then
i would've told you that you are magic
that there would be no home on earth
without your blessing
i would've signed off my promises with right action
given you a safe landing to fall
i would've sat at the end of the phone-line
helped you pack his bags for the last time
i would've painted the signs on billboards
met their tears with a dry face
i would've chosen your life over theirs
and showed you that punches
cannot deflower petals from a rose
but fire can create hell
for every advantage taken at your expense
i would've sacrificed me to give you
the chance to run wild and free
and i wouldn't have left you
with any
regrets

~ *women like you*
make the news

this time i'm leaving
this time tomorrow
there will be no sorrow
painting my face an age of grieving
this time i will trip guilts feet
before it knocks me back into
hollow conversations
trials and tribulations
allowing me the chance
to embrace congratulations
without my rewards being demanded
by entitled empty hands
that never lifted a tissue to wipe
a tear from the eyes with vision
no longer will
i take prescriptions
of crippling afflictions
that promise me disappointing twenty-fours
three sixty-five
roller coaster stomachs
and chakra's that close
as i arrive
this time
goodbye
for the first time
means goodbye

~ *i'm leaving*

on the mornings she beats sunset
birds relay what angels left at night
it's just enough hope
to face demons one more time

~ *every day is war*

there's a pain in her purse
that only the cause
knows the intensity
of which it
blunt forced wounds into her spirit

only those who wear lips tightly glued
with pride
could know the burdens planted
in a heart wedged open for them

and still spare apologies
from a soul bleeding for justice

one foot in the edge of this ditch
she dangles next to the feet of her Creator
for this moment she is safe
in faith

still seeping life on the floor
gasping for answers on the shore
til she feels no more

but they said hope was free
so she filled her cup

they called her greedy
she found greener grass with it half full

and the reflection in her tears
on the turf
show angels by her side

~ you know what you did

sometimes i lay in chills
and nearing spirits sing me lullabies
briefly, my mind creates an image of
the ancestor
holding me
i'm rocked out of thought to
simply embrace the tenderness
i've never felt from a living soul
i'm reminded that loneliness
is only skin deep

~ *held*

teardrops from the sky grace the leaves
colourful shades of green hold them
soon to be picked
for the mere purpose of pickings sake
never to be revered

may be seen as an object,
and made for
humans
purposeless desire

what is the rush
why do we have to have it before
intention settles within ourselves

what is so wrong with simple admiration
to look at a thing from afar
caress within our dreams
until alignment
from the step that we walk
to the tongue that we talk
is balanced enough to greet
what we have so longed to meet

what is the need for prematurity

why do we fear losing what is not even ours to begin,
what has never been ours to own

is that possible

to value the loss of an opportunity more than the truth of a person

what do we feel it says about us
if we allow an angel to walk past
without feeling the need to touch
to see if it's real

what does it say about us
that we print our fingers over glass
searching for validation
rather than just touching the skin we are in

why do we misvalue the reflection of ourselves
more than we value who we really are

why are we running
and what are we running from

i think the answers are rested in stillness

in true appreciation

in the bulge of our stomach when we hold our breath

in the exhale that allows our breaths to meet
the breath of those across the street

strangers

to blow as breeze
until the spring
offers
pink flowers
to the backdrop of the blue sky

the trees wave us
grand risings
and good morrows

the curiosity of nature
runs through our veins
takes in what it has known to be true
its whole life

weighs it against the weight of the world

the weight of so-called normalcy

cries like the sky
onto the leaves used for pickings sake

and then runs too
out of fear of being left behind

~ for the love of missing out

not broken
nor bent

bruised

at the ego
    and the heart

so, she ripped it out
   let pride bleed to its death
    til the purity of who her soul
      belonged to
        continued…

~ *dying to live*

the idea of healing sounds beautiful
'til you make it to the other side
and realise the comfort of delusion
is to believe what does not exist
and everything is simply
as your intuition guided you towards
every first time you chose to ignore it
you begin to find excitement in
things you cannot share
because there is nobody left
because when they say
everybody can't go
they mean
everybody
so it gets lonely at the top
probably why so many jump off buildings
before everybody returns to
assume they had it all
but if all is the understanding
that really nothing matters
all is not much to hold on to
to prevent a fall
i no longer have the care
to drift from cliffs
i'll stay
though never satisfied
at least when life made me sick
it left me deficient in hope
now everything feels possible
even the love that seemed a dream
and the emptiness of knowing
it still might not choose you

~ *ideas are distractions*

clipped wings fall
through galaxies
as the venusian woman sheds
the silence
once glued to
dimensions from home
she remembers herself
into the
stratosphere
of her
destiny
she welcomes life
and so it begins

~ *trading survival mode*

i learned to let go in the face of sorrow once ran from
took my soul out of the mould that slips
discreetly through cracks of humble visibility
and let it dance over albanian toes
a familiar strangers embrace
kissed away rigidity
dethroned last false ownership
on a last first date
in honour of boundaries
then allowed my pull to pour
free drinks for new friends
from barmen who appreciate the girl who
dances across fira town
with a mouth full of pistachio sorbet
bleeding hearts near oceans
under midnight breezes
sit in closed rooftop restaurants
in share of themselves
out of their shell
walks truth that resuscitates
the poet out of a martyr
reminded of a vow to set skin to sail
in effort to suffer in bare honesty
if ever to suffer again

~ *greek firsts*

i mixed spirits with pills
lay without gratitude
and asked you to take me
you took me out of parties
minutes before gunfire

i gave my last to friends
you closed my eyes with migraines
so, i could escape the sight of
knives placed in my back
pennies pinched from my purse

when i let my guard down
you placed bars around
those who wished me ill
healed my scars
and reimbursed every stolen pound
with roundtrips overseas

i lay my head on dead friends' bodies
you gave me warm hands
and life support to let go
you let me feel hurt
by what i love
teaching me not to hurt
who i love

in my saddest ages
visited with light shone by angels
placed same glow around me
to carry into rooms
for those who refuse to see you

i should've died over
until under was my only home
you left me with mere bruises
then sat me back on earths throne

and now i know why you keep blessing me
now i know why
now i know why

~ *her pain*

my self-compassion is reviewed
with each firmer step
into authentic presence
i am only that i am
still,
unlock my door to catalysts
mistaking of kin
'til what appeared sweet
turns out to be sour
and i remember
not to accept
what does not belong to me

~ *projections*

have you ever heard the moon sing?
exquisite does not suffice
the humming of mantra
awakening goddess from ancient depths
an invitation to harmonise with her
brings you to meet your own melody
the mask fades
veil thins
sacred chills twirl
your temple
to trance
the most beautiful tune begins
and it turns out to be
you

~ *child of the moon*

the pointlessness of a complaint
from a mystic knowing
makes a myth out of
all pain once endured

a myth so wished upon
in the face of moments
that would mark the
old heart who pondered
where joy was

searched for a peace
that would caress her heart
and cradle she

who aches in optimism
a longing finally found
yet rebuked in the name of suffering
that no longer defaults
but ignites the only bleed
to pour
wells of inspiration
from wounds to the soul

a receipt of a desire of much use
brings ease into the generations to become
if she so chooses to
set free from was
to be
the most foreign thing on earth
authentically present

without feeling
she is numb
     the home of her voice
to use it takes the exhalation she lives in now
only in it she finds
nothing to say
for in exhalation
she is that she is

~ *i am*

for God
loves me so
guided me through
heart aches
breaks
released distraction
of hell
on earth
stripped love
of flesh
til lonely
let soul love
self fluidly
left me
breathless
with only
itself
to rely
for God
loves me so
let me
make a mess of
its masterpiece
then gathered my
pieces and
brought me
home

~ *a creator's love*

akrotiri nights by the sea
conversing with strangers who see
the beyond of leon bridges
beneath a wandering british girl
i realise that mirrors are not ornaments
that return your outer experience to your eyes
but the human shells with
no similarities in skin or feature
yet everything in spirit alike
conduits of divinity relayed from the Creator
showing what you deny from intuitive visits
my heart sings a silent tune
i wonder if it is the same song
the man who just told me to
settle for no less than the
one who learns my dna
just danced to with his wife
at the bus station
he tells me she is unique
 i can tell
she returns his sentiments
    i see it well
my life would be in pieces in this moment
if a loving atmosphere
wasn't holding me together

~ *i forgot to ask his name*

outside of myself
i am reflected in simplicity

amused even at the thought of
a simple me

spontaneity and santorini
inspire *wish i could's*
and *you're so lucky's* from those
who know nothing of the many places
fighting for the presence of my heart

i am so torn
i almost feel together

life balances on my heart
with heavy feet that
knock the soul right into a feather
floating to look upon the
many things i am in this moment

both in love with life
 and haunted by a knife
the recurring state of my entire existence

 intensified by the unforgettable face
of a final end

the equation of putting pieces together
return a truth
that is ruth-
less i forget that answered prayers
are not always pretty
    the memory of now
            will not fail to remind me

~ *outsiders*

in the land of billions
who share same skin
it is the shadows
that fly past
the corner of her left eye
that take her away from
empty conversations
physical disconnection
the discomforting grazes
on her shell
take her away from
parched organs
starving for companionship
only ever able to conjure
same imagination of those
who create
film
to capture stories
that mark their loneliness as art

~ i should make a movie

tragic little muse
lonely beyond the idea
others find infatuation with
your dreams are your flair
inspiring those who only ever
lived in nightmares
to flip pillows and drift
into cool peace
to turn frowns into smiles
and make a home of this world
an unfulfilling purpose that makes
life no longer feel lonely
to those that tick you into boxes
limiting you to where they
decided you were perfect
you wonder if they know
there's more to you than that
poor thing,
they don't care
once you're propped onto their special shelf
never to be touched again
'cause God forbid you break her

i would rather be broken
trodded on and used
like an infant's favourite blanket
that a parent better not lose
i've never been anyone's favourite
anyone would beg to differ
i say they're all too busy thinking
i've got options
and i do
if you're to call
admirers across all lands
options
in my eyes
picking from vessels
that only see you
as deep as themselves
when that is truly never deep at all
is an option i'd trade for
a shoulder to cry on
the freedom to make a mistake
and the experience of being felt
past desire

~ *anyday*

maybe there's more to me
than meets my sight
maybe just i am blind
and what they see is true
that along with all the pain
i have too earned glory

~ *maybe*

i'm used to running away on planes
people look at me for my chutzpah
call me brave
maybe
brave to withstand the pain that i'm running from
brave to not run more often
you see,
bravery is in the heart of who beholds it
on the outside, my escapes look like
visiting places where you know nothing but yourself
to me, that is not frightening
to i who have faced monsters
when i step out of the sky
into countries that do not know my name
i face bliss
i am only alone at home
surrounded by people
who have experienced me to comfortability
from the outside looking in
one would assume they know me
they don't
sands that i walk in for the first time
hold me better than people who have
laid their head on my shoulder
bled their tears down to my fingertips
i belong to them at home
but when i wander
i get to be mine

~ *just me*

sensuous priestess
bounded to borders
that save weak men
from being enamoured
deeper than the layer of
instant infatuation
following the sirens melody
alone,
her aura gives rise
to divinity in masculines
who only ever existed in
empty casings
awakens enough life
for them to reach
contentment in a carbon copy
and doesn't grant them
the luck to taste
as she swore
not to capture any
slaves
in this lifetime

~ *sacred siren*

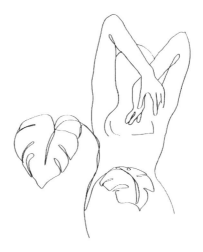

i belong to the cosmic mothers
of lotus bloomed rivers
the sensitive senses who
in the noise of crowds
hear God's whispers
the reminders
who first had to lose their way
to realise they were never lost
my spirit guides leave my side
to greet their tribe
as i await their return
i meet my family in the
stranger's eyes
waiting for their trusted
to release embrace from mine
i hum my mother tongue
under human breath
and sacred language
meets ears that do not fall deaf
it is easy
after it is ever hard
in the moments i sullenly lay
the divine places crossroads
on my path
there i bump into being held
without a bind
it is the souls that see me without
tallying my expense
that i know are home to me

~ *soul family*

my holy room is a garden
where angels walk freely
pathways are paved
with mosaic stones
i ground my feet into their cracks
amethyst hugs my roots
as fresh cords replace
open wounds
i see my children
in my grandfather's arms
and smile with friends
who are no longer dead
the peace of my praying heart
blows through the trees
and i hear the answers to my asking
before questions fall from my lips
i died to my flesh
and woke up in heaven
i found my inheritance
in that holy room

~ *my sanctuary*

the day i stopped
lying to myself
i learned
me and my mother
are the same person
and when i love us
she can love her
too

~ *wednesday women*

to the women with vision
led by the One unseen

   the mystic martyrs
so aware of the power of their prayers
that words of illness no longer
fall from their lips

the sisters rebuking
the cursing that beholds generations

to the dancers of intuition
who evade demons
to the appearance of craziness

the seers; doers.
labelled, abused, and accused,

the ears that hear divinity
and answer callings
the self-qualified
cannot comprehend

to the women demanding with faith
that the weights before us
must let God's
people go

the harriet's and joan's
the princesses of egypt

welcome home

~ *sacred return*

she is the unseen
the relied on
the being called in in prayer
by ancestors cast out
far enough for God to show its face
she is the forceful destroyer
of disguises
that hold eyes hostage
from your own light
she remembers
and when she graces you with her presence
you remember too
and you begin to see her as the seer
for she is
and the seer you begin to see everywhere
for she is
and if you are not tamed by her
you will be afraid at the promise her existence makes
and run away from yourself
she is adhesive
so far as you run
she does not leave
if you fear God you will believe she haunts you
will paint her in hues of green
and sell her to be hung under
accusations of witchcraft
all who also know not love will burn her at the stake
you will see the forgiveness in her eyes
as she continues to ash
and it will be you who feels crucified
the mystic has been you
is you still
only she knows the mystery of life
and will not depart until you do, too

~ *the mystic and her marathon*

caught up in the joie
de vivre
twinkle toes full of
caribbean sand
trail me to british
bedsheets
giggles from strangers'
shoulders
reheat the bottles that
warm cramps
and everywhere
i am safe
i poke my tongue out
and taste the aroma
of today
a gift that never goes
out of date
my mistakes sound like
visa från utanmyra
i savour the instants
cheeks scratch pavements
more than the era i'll rise again
i leave lula mae barnes in doc's memory
pick myself a face that sleeps under a smile
and i'm born thirty years my senior
when newspapers get away with telling lies
and decide i'll tell my own
i take art out of my head
and style a ball gown with the cash
i strut streets like a black-and-white movie star
in between the breaks of time
my brown skin is the sun
and no matter what happens tomorrow
it will be in truth
that i spent sundry days of my life
truly alive

~ it was always my story

final labour

in my darkest hours
the light of me dances upon the grave
of the shell i once carried

under this world is a home
that treacherous experiences initiate me into
each time i pull too far from my truth

the strength of me is not to be ignored
is not to be diminished or traded for vulnerability
but is a superpower that although afforded
should be spent sparingly

see, i am a frugal Goddess,
that which takes care of me
showers me in the abundance of peace
covers me in glory
sees the faults that i bury under flowers
and turns my eyes to the beauty that blooms
when i seek to bow my head

in this final labour
i give birth to the worries that are to come
cradle them in my arms
look at the expression of missions
i would have aborted in shame
and hold them to the sun as royalty

from me to you

i give the parts of myself
i refuse to judge anymore
the parts of myself that deny
the morale i uphold on most days
yet act as if they don't exist

on days where my dreams come to fruition
in ways that i didn't expect
i pray prayers and beg for them to be answered again
but in my language
forgetting that God is teaching me tongues
to provide the highest good for all

i have wept in secret
on floors that carry the rivers and oceans
of the deepest sorrow
rooted in the anatomy of my pelvis

i thought they tried to bury me alive
so i ran from them
so far that i ran also from
the actions that i took
and the fact that it was me who lay myself there

this final labour sees the little light
that could do nothing but shine
in the forest of perversion
rip shame bare from the skin
tear it to a bleed
and burn every hand that touched it
without consent

forms a lotus prayer in palm
forgives myself for calling in judgment
i should never care for
accepts the losses that do not come with new lessons
but reinstate the most valuable

i had to fall again
everything i would've laid my life down for
had to fall from me
because the underworld summons for me to live here

lightening rages across the seas
on the days that i choose to worry
the earth quakes beneath me
when i do not nurture my worth

i will look around in this court of
social acceptance again
still wonder what i'm doing here

cause somewhere along the way
i chose that i liked someone else's movie better
and moulded myself into their experience

and then i did it time and time again
'til i became everything but
the darling who lays alone at night
gives thanks for everybody else first
turns her back to the sight of the sacred within
whilst angels cry over her shoulder

love is a labour
it is tiresome, gruesome
it is a fight to let go of all chains
that would surely hang a soul
or beat it black and blue
if lip corners curl wide enough to
proclaim authentic power
without seeking validation

it is a labour worth the battle

i meet my labour with vision
see pyramids that if to be filled with tombs
are left with etchings of beauty
that descended generations will follow
and be proud that

by the divine
the indelible mark i chose to leave here
was not lost in the quarters of honesty
that once existed
when stories were kept silenced

this final labour says hello to legacy
welcome's her back with fresh eyes
and allows her to introduce herself
this time
in her own right

~ *final labour*

acknowledgments

thank you to the fullness, mistakes, awakenings, courage, fear, joy, grief, wanders, teachers, spirit guides, love, and kitchen floor full of tears that have been on this walk with me

thank you to the ancestors that etched my path

thank you to my unborn children that i do it all for

thank you to myself for being brave enough to exist only in honesty

most sacredly,

thank you God, for governing everything that i have to be thankful for and sitting with me when you could be anywhere else in the world

Printed in Great Britain
by Amazon

78564784R00064